100

THINGS TO DO IN
DALLAS
FORT WORTH
BEFORE YOU
DIE

...dition

D1468484

100

THINGS TO DO IN
DALLAS
FORT WORTH
BEFORE YOU
DIE

• •

TUI SNIDER

REEDY PRESS

2nd Edition

Library of Congress Control Number: 2018945639

ISBN: 9781681061702

Design by Jill Halpin

Printed in the United States of America
18 19 20 21 22   5 4 3 2 1

Please note that websites, phone numbers, addresses, and company names are subject to change or cancellation. We did our best to relay the most accurate information available, but due to circumstances beyond our control, please do not hold us liable for misinformation. When exploring new destinations, please do your homework before you go.

DEDICATION

To Larry: Wherever I go, it's home when you're there!

To my supportive newsletter readers: I'm so grateful
for your input and did my best to squeeze
all your favorite DFW places into this book!

• •

CONTENTS

Music and Entertainment

• •

● ●

● ●

• •

• •

ACKNOWLEDGMENTS

While so many people help me with every book I write, this time I owe extra special thanks to Teal Gray, David Kravetz, Donna and Joe Sanchez, Pat and Russell Snider, Kristine Hall, Linda Hill, Katherine Boyer, and the #StoryDam crew on Twitter for your timely advice, suggestions, and much-needed support while writing this book!

PREFACE

Sometimes the hardest part of travel is simply getting out the door. For instance, have you ever drawn a blank when a friend or family member asks, "What do you want to do today?" Maybe you have out-of-town guests and find yourself stymied when they ask you to show them around the Dallas-Fort Worth Metroplex. Or perhaps you've lived here for years and feel like you're in a rut, doing the exact same things every weekend rather than experiencing anything new.

If so, this book is for you! If you live in, or are visiting, the DFW region, this list will inspire you to start exploring. If you're hungry, flip through the Food and Drink section. Looking for entertainment or want to get outdoors? Dig into the Music and Entertainment or the Sports and Recreation sections. Want to barter for antiques or see a museum? Check out the Culture and History or the Shopping and Fashion sections. In the back of the book, you'll also find suggested itineraries as well as seasonal items.

This book is meant to spark ideas—everything from family outings, date nights, and solo excursions, to simply hanging out with friends. It contains places you can visit on a whim as well as festivals and events you will need to plan for in advance.

Have fun with it!

I certainly had a blast researching places to include, although I'm the first to admit that this list is merely the tip of the iceberg.

• •

There wasn't room to include every single wonderful thing to see and do around here, although I tried. I really did!

Also, I'd like to clarify that this book includes places all over the Dallas-Fort Worth Metroplex. In other words, there's much more to it than venues in Dallas and Fort Worth. While those two cities are heavily represented, the DFW Metroplex includes twelve counties spread across 9,286 square miles. That's a larger area than the entire states of Rhode Island and Connecticut—combined. So it's simply impossible to do the Dallas-Fort Worth Metroplex justice with a list of only one hundred things.

In fact, since my original list included nearly three hundred items, the most challenging part of this project was deciding which ones to leave out! When deciding what to include, I chose to showcase venues that have withstood the test of time. Not only are these places more likely to stay in business after publication, but they are also more likely to feature prominently in the memories of those who grew up in North Texas.

In fact, several of those who subscribe to my weekly author newsletter were eager to share lists of their favorite DFW places—places they visited as a child and that they now return to with their own children or grandchildren. To me, these are the places that best belong on a bucket list—places deeply woven into personal travel memories created with friends and family. I hope this book inspires you to get out there and make some lasting travel memories of your own.

• •

Breakfast at GINGER'S

GINGER BROWN'S

est. 1985

Presented in TEGGNICOLOR

A **Dazzling Dining** Experience at the **only place** where **Cinnamon Rolls** are a **Girl's Best Friend!**

World Famous Homemade Cinnamon Rolls

FOOD AND DRINK

GET STICKY FINGERS
AT GINGER BROWN'S OLD TYME RESTAURANT & BAKERY

Ginger Brown's Old Tyme Restaurant & Bakery is a local institution that's been dishing up hefty portions of Southern-style comfort food for more than thirty years. Don't be surprised if the friendly waitstaff treats you like family and calls you "honey" as they top off your coffee or tea. Each entree comes with one of Ginger's legendary cinnamon rolls as a bonus. The walls are lined with historic photos as well as playful cinnamon roll advertisements featuring Ginger Brown herself. In one she wears her sticky buns à la Princess Leia for "Star Rolls," and in another she's dressed like Audrey Hepburn for "Breakfast at Ginger's." On Tuesdays, first responders and members of the military get 50 percent off, and the same goes for teachers and school staff on Wednesdays.

6312 Jacksboro Hwy., Fort Worth
817-237-2114
gingerbrowns.com

SAVOR A GAME CHANGER
AT CLEBURNE'S BURGER BAR

Since 1949 this tiny brick building has dished up delicious burgers and fries to eager locals in downtown Cleburne. How good are they? In 2014, Burger Bar won the Gameday Burger Battle judged by none other than Food Network celebrity Guy Fieri. The menu at Burger Bar is simple: burgers, fries, and soft drinks. For a taste of their award-winning burger, order "The Game Changer." The joint only seats four, but a picnic table is also outside. The Burger Bar is a beloved local institution, and its current co-owner, Katy Grantges, has been flipping burgers here since she was fifteen. If you're looking for a hearty bacon burger with a hefty side of small-town charm, look no further!

109 N. Anglin St., Cleburne
817-645-9031
facebook.com/burgerbar49/

GRAB TEXAS BY THE GRAPES
ALONG THE DALLAS TOWN & COUNTRY WINE TRAIL

Many North Texas wineries urge visitors to "Come grab Dallas by the grapes!" To assist with this, eight wineries in the DFW Metroplex combine forces to create the Dallas Town & Country Wine Trail, a group that organizes festive wine tasting events throughout the year. A Wine Trail ticket includes a souvenir glass along with the chance to visit several different wineries for one fee. Whether you choose to visit all in one day or spread your trips over the course of a weekend or several days, remember to designate a driver. The staff at each winery will not only offer tours of their facilities and wine tastings, but they are also happy to suggest places to eat or stay while you explore.

dallastownandcountrywinetrail.com

LIST OF ALL EIGHT WINERIES ON THE TRAIL:

Carmela Winery
132 N. Louisiana Dr., Celina
844-227-9463, carmelawinery.net

Caudalie Crest Winery
2045 Weston Rd., Celina
214-578-6390, goatsngrapes.com

Eden Hill Winery
4910 Eden Hill Ln., Celina
214-850-4081, edenhill.com

Fortunata Winery
2297 FM 2931, Aubrey
940-440-9463, fortunatawinery.com

Grayson Hills Winery
2815 Ball Rd., Whitewright
903-627-0832, graysonhillswinery.com

Landon Winery (McKinney)
101 N. Kentucky St., McKinney
972-542-3030, landonwinery.com

Landon Winery (Wylie)
103 N. Ballard Ave., Wylie
972-442-0155, landonwinery.com

Lone Star Wine Cellars
103 E. Virginia St., McKinney
972-547-9463, lonestarwinecellars.com

FEAST AT A TABLE SET FOR 300
AT PLANO'S NIGHT OUT ON 15TH STREET

Imagine a busy city street closed to through traffic so that a 300-foot-long table may be set for a gourmet meal. That's exactly what happens on Fifteenth Street, located in the heart of Plano's arts district, each June. Chefs from several revered eateries participate in this unique communal event. Many use the Night Out on 15th Street as a chance to debut new menu items. These chefs collaborate to create a special event featuring sumptuous entrees paired with beer, wine, and booze. This includes a cocktail reception before the sit-down meal. Live musicians fill the air with dinner music during the meal itself. Afterward, you can enjoy a whiskey tasting and cigar selection al fresco courtesy of Mercedes-Benz of Plano. Proceeds benefit the Scottish Rite Hospital for Children.

998 E. Fifteenth St., Plano
visitdowntownplano.com/night-out-on-15th

RUSTLE UP SOME GRUB
AT A COWTOWN STEAKHOUSE

Up until the mid-1950s, Fort Worth was the biggest livestock market south of Kansas City. They don't call Fort Worth "Cowtown" for nothing, and there's no shortage of good steak restaurants to be found. Here are a few worth trying: For farm-to-market freshness and locally sourced wild game, try Bonnell's Fine Texas Cuisine. For an old-school corn-fed steak at a place that's been around since 1947, head to Cattlemen's Fort Worth Steak House. For a hearty steak in historic Sundance Square, choose Del Frisco's Double Eagle Steak House. For a sophisticated and modern take, try Grace, where local ingredients are the focus, and your steak comes from grass-fed cows.

Bonnell's Fine Texas Cuisine
4259 Bryant Irvin Rd.,
Fort Worth
817-738-5489
bonnellstexas.com

Del Frisco's Double Eagle
Steak House
812 Main St., Fort Worth
817-877-3999
delfriscos.com/steakhouse/fort-worth

Cattlemen's Fort Worth Steak House
2458 N. Main St., Fort Worth
817-624-3945
cattlemenssteakhouse.com

Grace
777 Main St., Fort Worth
817-877-3388
gracefortworth.com

DISCOVER WHY GOGO GUMBO!
PUTS BOYD ON THE MAP

Calling itself "the fancy place in Boyd," is more than just a tongue-in-cheek jab; Gogo Gumbo! has really put this small North Texas town on the map. By dishing out meals to more than 1,300 patrons each week, the number of people Gogo Gumbo! feeds exceeds the entire population of Boyd. In 2008, chef Kraig Thome and his wife, Letty, moved up from Houston to open a Cajun-influenced restaurant where everything is made from scratch. Within a few months, word of mouth brought so much business that pagers are needed to deal with the overflow from their fifty-seat venue. Ten years later, diehard fans from all over the Metroplex happily wait out on the sidewalk for their turn to experience the gourmet offerings inside.

116 W. Rock Island Ave., Boyd
940-433-3474
gogogumbo.com

NOSH ON TEX-MEX OR ITALIAN
WITH A MID-CENTURY VIBE
AT CANDLELITE INN

When the Candlelite Inn first opened its doors in 1957, it was the first restaurant in Arlington to serve pizza. They soon added Tex-Mex, steak, and Italian items to their menu. Today, it's a great place to take your family for lunch or dinner because you don't have to settle on just one style of cuisine. The Candlelite Inn was recently remodeled by current owners, Alan and Bonnie Petsche, who made updates and improvements (such as a bar and banquet rooms) while carefully preserving the Candlelite Inn's mid-century vibe, including its dimly lit booths, red-and-white checked table cloths, and the iconic neon candle-shaped signage out front. Head here the next time one of you craves a burrito and the other wants chicken parmigiana.

1202 E. Division St., Arlington
817-275-9613
candleliteinnarlington.com

TREAT YOURSELF TO A MEAL
BY THE BIG D'S CELEBRITY CHEFS

If you're ready to splash out some cash, consider a meal at some of the swankier venues the Big D offers. From Blythe Beck (host of *The Naughty Kitchen*), Dean Fearing (deemed Best Chef in the Southwest by the James Beard Foundation), Stephan Pyles (AAA Five Diamond Award winner), and Kent Rathbun (*Iron Chef America* winner), these restaurants with celebrity chefs at the helm are sure to impress your date.

Blythe Beck - Pink Magnolia
642 W Davis St., Dallas
469-320-9220
pinkmagnoliadallas.com

Stephan Pyles - Flora Street Café
2330 Flora St., Ste. 150, Dallas
214-580-7000
florastreet.com

Dean Fearing - Fearing's
2121 McKinney Ave.
Dallas
214-922-4848
fearingsrestaurant.com

Stampede 66 - Stephen Pyles
1717 McKinney Ave., Ste. 100,
Dallas
214-550-6966
stampede66restaurant.com

Kent Rathbun - Abacus
4511 McKinney Ave., Dallas
214-559-3111
abacusjaspers.com

DO THE HOKEY POKEY
AT BABE'S CHICKEN DINNER HOUSE

The first Babe's Chicken Dinner House opened in Roanoke in 1993. Since then the restaurant has expanded to include nine locations throughout the DFW Metroplex. Each Babe's has slightly different decor and entree options, but much is the same. First off, there's no paper menu. You simply choose between chicken or chicken fried steak (some locations include catfish, smoked chicken, and more). Next, your server brings several sides, including mashed potatoes, green beans, biscuits, creamed corn, and a very basic salad. If you want seconds on any of those sides, just ask. Some locations don't offer dessert, but a fresh biscuit with melted butter and sorghum syrup is just as satisfying. Servers dance to the hokey pokey when it is played. You and your kids are welcome to join in.

104 N. Oak St., Roanoke
817-491-2900
babeschicken.com

SAVE ROOM FOR STRUDEL
AT LITTLE GERMANY RESTAURANT

Little Germany Restaurant is a cozy hole-in-the-wall where you can enjoy German dishes, including sauerbraten, spaetzle, goulash, potato pancakes, bratwurst, red cabbage, sauerkraut, schnitzel, imported German beer, and much more. Don't worry if you're not familiar with German fare. The friendly waitstaff here will guide you through the menu and help you find something tasty to enjoy. Save room for the apple strudel à la mode if you can. Whatever you do, bring your appetite because portions are hearty.

Little Germany
703 N. Henderson St., Fort Worth
682-224-2601
littlegermanyfortworth.com

TIP
Starting in the 1830s, tens of thousands of Germans entered the United States through the Port of Galveston. While the German flag never flew over Texas, its language and food are deeply woven into the cultural fabric. Not only can you find German bakeries, delis, and restaurants throughout the state, but Texas also has its own unique German dialect. Learn more at the Texas German Dialect Project: tgdp.org

TWO MORE GERMAN RESTAURANTS TO TRY:

Edelweiss German Restaurant
(Often has live German music)
3801 Southwest Blvd., Fort Worth
817-738-5934
edelweissgermanrestaurant.com

Ketzler's Schnitzel Haus & Biergarten
(Live music and an outdoor beer garden)
101 E. Pearl St., Granbury
682-936-2777
ketzlersschnitzelhaus.com

DRIVE THROUGH A TRUE AMERICAN DRIVE-IN
AT THE MALT SHOP

The Malt Shop is an old-time burger joint that has been a Weatherford mainstay since 1958, with picnic tables out front covered in decades-old graffiti and hand-carved initials to prove it. The menu here is simple: burgers, fries, onion rings, Frito pie, real ice cream shakes, and, of course, malts. This is a true American drive-in. Place your order at the window and then wait in your car or sit at a picnic table until it's ready. Every Monday after 5:00 p.m. burgers are half-price. In 2017, the Malt Shop changed hands, but there's no need to worry that it will change character because the new owner, Janie Williams, worked there for thirty years before buying it. This is a fun place to go for a taste of vintage Americana.

2038 Fort Worth Hwy. (US 180), Weatherford
817-594-2524

SAVOR GOURMET VEGETARIAN FOOD
AT KALACHANDJI'S RESTAURANT AND PALACE

Kalachandji's Restaurant and Palace is tucked in an eye-catching Hare Krishna temple. Its ornate onion-domed exterior is a surprising sight in the middle of a humble neighborhood. Gourmet vegetarian meals are served buffet style, with an authentic Indian menu that changes daily. The cuisine is not only meatless but also contains no eggs, onion, or garlic. Despite these restrictions, the dishes are flavorful and varied. While Kalachandji's is a longtime favorite with locals, many famous visitors have dropped by through the years. The hallway is lined with magazine reviews and autographed photos from the likes of Peter Gabriel, Billy Corgan, and Todd Rundgren. A thank-you letter from Annie Lennox reads in part: "You have created an oasis in this desert of slaughterhouses."

5430 Gurley Ave., Dallas
214-821-1048
kalachandjis.com

DELIGHT IN TEX-MEX ALFRESCO
AT JOE T. GARCIA'S

Established in 1935, Joe T. Garcia's is a Fort Worth institution. This Tex-Mex restaurant started with seating for sixteen and has grown to accommodate well over a thousand. Joe T's is a cash-only restaurant that doesn't bother with a printed menu since only two options are available: fajitas or enchiladas. Before you go, take heed. Unless you enjoy crowds and long waits, this place is best experienced during the middle of the week; otherwise it's mobbed, and parking is a challenge. When timed right, however, a trip to Joe T. Garcia's is a wonderful respite. The garden patio is enormous and beautifully landscaped, with statues, archways, mosaics, and fountains throughout. They have heaters for the winter and fans for the summer, so it's definitely worth sitting outside.

2201 N. Commerce St., Fort Worth
817-626-4356
joetgarcias.com

WITNESS GERMAN PANCAKE "ORIGAMI"
AT OL' SOUTH PANCAKE HOUSE

Ol' South Pancake House is a crowd-pleasing place that consistently wins awards for "best breakfast in Fort Worth." This local landmark was established in 1962 and is an after-church tradition for many. Since Ol' South is open twenty-four hours, you can easily avoid crowds and long waits by visiting during off hours. Although the extensive menu offers a wide range of traditional Southern comfort foods (fried squash, chicken fried steak, black-eyed peas, catfish, and chicken fried chicken), their German Pancakes are a unique tradition and not to be missed. Your server finishes this tasty creation at your table by squeezing lemons, dusting it with powdered sugar, and then folding it into a neat little square of yumminess for you to enjoy.

1509 S. University Dr., Fort Worth
817-336-0311
olsouthpancakehouse.com

TASTE WORLD-FAMOUS FRUITCAKE
AT COLLIN STREET BAKERY

It's a good thing Gus Weidmann remembered to bring his family recipes along when he emigrated to Texas. In 1896, he opened a bakery in Corsicana. A chance visit from John Ringling's circus troupe thrust him into the mail order business. The circus folks asked him to send fruitcakes to their families all across Europe, so he obliged. More than a century later, Collin Street Bakery still ships fruitcakes to 196 countries and all fifty states! These days, in addition to their award-winning, world-famous fruitcake, Collin Street Bakery offers an outstanding array of soups, sandwiches, and sumptuous baked goods. If you can't make up your mind, they are generous with samples to help you decide.

401 W. Seventh Ave., Corsicana
903-874-7477
collinstreet.com

BITE INTO
HAND-FORMED PATTIES
WITH A SIDE OF KITSCH AT
CLOWN HAMBURGERS TOO

Although the official business name is "Clown Hamburgers Too," locals simply refer to this Haltom City restaurant as "Clown Burger." Since 1959, the specialty here has been thin burger patties and hand-cut French fries. The ambience is kitchsy and eclectic, with a few clowns here and there, as you might expect. Elvis fans will enjoy the decor. There's a shrine to the King of Rock and Roll in the front room, and you'll often hear his songs coming through the speakers if you choose to dine in. My favorite place to sit is in the section of graffiti-laden booths called the Belknap Room. Although the man who ran the place for fifty-three years recently retired, his daughter is now in charge, so Clown Burger has stayed in the family.

5020 Stanley Keller Rd., Haltom City
817-298-1477
facebook.com/clownburger

TUCK INTO COWBOY FARE WITH A CHIC TWIST
AT LONESOME DOVE WESTERN BISTRO

The city of Fort Worth prides itself for being a place where cowboys and culture meet. Perhaps no eatery exemplifies this better than the Lonesome Dove Western Bistro. Since 2000, award-winning chef Tim Love has been serving up traditional cowboy fare with a sophisticated twist. Where else are you going to find elk sausage sliders, rabbit, wild boar, kangaroo, and rattlesnake paired with habanero-fig sauce and other surprising creations on the menu? Don't be intimidated by the fancy fare. The servers will guide you through the menu options and help you choose well. The Lonesome Dove Western Bistro is perfect for a romantic night out or to celebrate a special occasion with a memorable meal.

2406 N. Main St., Fort Worth
817-740-8810
lonesomedovefortworth.com

REVEL IN RETRO MENU SPECIALTIES
AT HIGHLAND PARK SODA FOUNTAIN

The Highland Park Soda Fountain has been around since 1912, and folks, this place is the real deal, a genuine old-fashioned soda fountain, where servers are called "soda jerks," food is served on vintage dining ware, and there's a long counter with a row of stools. Everything here is reasonably priced. Beverages offered include milk shakes, malts, floats, egg creams, and phosphates. While some of the more retro sandwich offerings (such as ham salad, pimento cheese, and goose liver) may seem odd to modern folk, you can't go wrong ordering the house specialty, a good old-fashioned grilled cheese.

3229 Knox St., Dallas
214-521-2126
highlandparksodafountain.com

MUSIC AND ENTERTAINMENT

OGLE THE USA'S LARGEST COLLECTION
OF ART DECO BUILDINGS AT FAIR PARK

Not only is Fair Park the biggest historic landmark in Texas, but this 277-acre expanse also offers a wide variety of things to see and do. There's a planetarium, an outdoor amphitheater, The Dallas Aquarium, The Cotton Bowl, an IMAX Theater, swan-shaped paddle boats, the Music Hall at Fair Park (where you can see opera, ballet, and Broadway shows), and several museums. More than a hundred festivals and events take place on the grounds of Fair Park each year, including the granddaddy of them all, the Texas State Fair. Fair Park also features the largest collection of art deco buildings in the USA, with eye-catching murals, facades, and other architectural details adorning a series of exhibit halls built for the 1936 Texas Centennial Celebration hosted here.

1300 Robert B. Cullum Blvd., Dallas
214-670-8400
fairpark.org

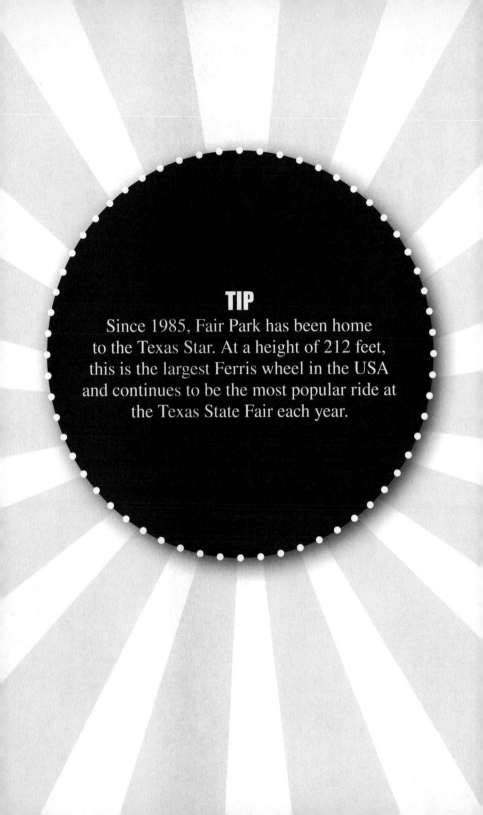

TIP

Since 1985, Fair Park has been home
to the Texas Star. At a height of 212 feet,
this is the largest Ferris wheel in the USA
and continues to be the most popular ride at
the Texas State Fair each year.

SCOOT YOUR BOOTS
THROUGH THE WORLD'S LARGEST
HONKY TONK, BILLY BOB'S TEXAS

The building housing Billy Bob's Texas started out as an open-air barn in 1910. In 1981, it was transformed into the world's largest honky tonk. Now it's so big that when Merle Haggard ordered a round of drinks for the house it took 5,095 shots of whisky to fill his order and set a world record. Besides two stages and three dance floors, a gift shop, pool tables, and arcade games, Billy Bob's features memorabilia from musicians and Western-style decor throughout. Every Friday and Saturday night Billy Bob's hosts a championship bull riding competition at their indoor arena. (And, yes, the bulls are real, not mechanical, although there's a stuffed bull for photo ops.)

2520 Rodeo Plaza, Fort Worth
817-624-7117
billybobstexas.com

A FEW OTHER PLACES TO SCOOT YOUR BOOTS ACROSS A WESTERN DANCE HALL:

Gilley's Dallas
1135 S. Lamar St., Dallas
214-421-2021
gilleysdallas.com

Stagecoach Ballroom
2516 E. Belknap St., Fort Worth
817-831-2261
stagecoachballroom.com

Southern Junction
101 N. Rogers Rd., Irving
469-417-0902
southernjunctionlive.com/irving

PARTY LIKE IT'S 1533
AT SCARBOROUGH
RENAISSANCE FESTIVAL

Each year from early April through the end of May the Scarborough Renaissance Festival comes to life across thirty-five acres on the outskirts of Waxahachie, with a cast of costumed characters reenacting life in the year 1533. With more than two hundred "shoppes" and constant entertainment across several stages, you simply cannot see it all in one day. Anne Boleyn and Henry VIII hold court, lead medieval dances, parades, and occasionally mingle with common folk. Special events occur each weekend, such as caber tossing, falconry, jugglers, jousts, and live music. There is plenty to learn from craftspeople who demonstrate the old ways. As you wander through the village, you will observe costumed artisans engaged in blacksmithing, glassblowing, candlemaking, and more. This lively Texas Renaissance festival has been a regional favorite since it first opened in 1981.

2511 FM 66, Waxahachie
srfestival.com

BOGGLE YOUR MIND
WITH THE LIVING BLACK & WHITE
AT PEGASUS THEATRE

Each winter Pegasus Theatre presents a unique production at the Eisemann Center in Richardson, Texas: a play that looks and feels like an old black-and-white movie. Through special trademarked makeup techniques, carefully chosen costuming, clever lighting, and stylized acting, the effect is so convincing that when a woman in a bright red dress steps onto the stage after the curtain call, it's jarring to the eyes. These Living Black & White productions are set in the 1930s and '40s. The storylines are tongue-in-cheek parodies of film noir and hard-boiled detective movies. Photography is not allowed during the performance, but afterward actors are available for photos in the lobby.

2351 Performance Dr., Richardson
214-821-6005
pegasustheatre.org

ENJOY WORLD-CLASS ACOUSTICS
AT THE BASS PERFORMANCE HALL

Thanks to a pair of forty-eight-foot trumpet-blowing angels jutting from its outside walls, Bass Performance Hall makes a striking sight in downtown Fort Worth. This venue, which first opened in 1998, is the permanent home to several performance companies, including the Fort Worth Opera, the Fort Worth Symphony Orchestra, Texas Ballet Theater, and the Van Cliburn International Piano Competition and Cliburn Concerts. Bass Hall is renowned for phenomenal acoustics, and it's often claimed there are no bad seats in the house. Free parking is easy to find nearby, and afterward you can stroll through picturesque Sundance Square. If you're looking for a sophisticated date night, look no further!

525 Commerce St., Fort Worth
817-212-4200
basshall.com

GAIN PERSPECTIVE
AT THE REUNION TOWER GeO-DECK

Like Seattle's Space Needle, Reunion Tower is an iconic and eye-catching shape along the city skyline in Dallas. At a height of 470 feet, the views here are tremendous. Touch screen monitors on the viewing deck let visitors leave their name and geographical information as well as email a free souvenir photo to themselves. Several ticket options are available, including one that lets you enjoy the view during the day and then return at night to enjoy the city lights. There is a gift shop for souvenir hunters, and after dark the Reunion Tower features a colorful light show. For special occasions, consider dinner or happy hour drinks in one of the rotating restaurants: Cloud Nine Café or Wolfgang Puck's Five Sixty. Diners are not required to purchase a GeO-Deck ticket.

300 Reunion Blvd. E., Dallas
214-712-7040
reuniontower.com

HAVE A BANG-UP TIME
AT ADDISON KABOOM TOWN!

Although Independence Day celebrations featuring fireworks displays take place all across the DFW Metroplex, the city of Addison takes this to a whole new level with its annual Kaboom Town event, which is ranked the No. 2 Independence Day fireworks display in America by yahoo.com and lauded by many others, including *USA Today*, *The Wall Street Journal*, and the American Pyrotechnic Association. The entertainment begins well before the actual fireworks display with live music, an air show, and a general festival vibe. Admission is free, but seating is first come, first served. A good strategy is to pack a picnic (don't forget drinks and sunscreen) and stake out our your viewing area as soon as the doors open at 4:00 p.m.

4970 Addison Circle Dr., Addison
972-450-2851
addisonkaboomtown.com

CUT A RUG
AT THE SONS OF HERMANN HALL

This popular venue was erected in 1910 by German settlers as a meeting place for the Sons of Hermann fraternal order. It has since become a Texas Historic Landmark and continues to function as a friendly neighborhood bar, rental hall, and performance venue for a variety of acts, ranging from classic country to rock and even stand-up comedy. On Wednesdays, you can sing karaoke and/or join a lively swing dance session. Can't dance? Show up early for a free swing lesson. On Thursdays, the venue hosts the "Electric Campfire Jam," an open mic for musicians of all ages and skill levels. If you take photos at the Sons of Hermann Hall, check them closely for misty apparitions and orbs. This place is widely regarded as a haunted hot spot!

3414 Elm St., Dallas
214-747-4422
sonsofhermann.com

CATCH A SHOW AT THE RIDGLEA, AN ART DECO LANDMARK

Erected in 1947, this art deco building in Fort Worth's Camp Bowie neighborhood nearly met the wrecking ball a few years back. The Ridglea has since been restored to its former glory, including its original terrazzo tile floor, seventy-foot stone tower, and unique Spanish-Mediterranean architectural details throughout. This historic Fort Worth landmark now offers three different event spaces within its 20,000-square-feet expanse. The Ridglea Theater, which boasts the largest traditional movie screen in the area, shows films, and The Ridglea Lounge and The Ridglea Room are where you can catch live acts, ranging from big band and cabaret to alternative rock and blues. While all three Ridglea venues are available for private events, they offer public events, including themed parties, live music, and comedy throughout the year.

6025 Camp Bowie Blvd., Fort Worth
817-738-9500
theridglea.com

KICK OFF THE HALLOWEEN SEASON
AT THE GRANBURY PARANORMAL EXPO

If you're a fan of TV's ghost hunting shows, here's an event for you: The Granbury Paranormal Expo is an annual two-day street festival that takes place over the last weekend of September in the historic town square of Granbury. This family-friendly gathering is free to the public and a great way to celebrate the start of Halloween season. Each year attendees can hear speakers, including celebrity ghost hunters, horror actors, authors, and more. Food and drinks are available on-site, along with an assortment of vendors selling ghost hunting equipment, books, clothing, artwork, handcrafted items, spooky dolls, and even Tarot card and other psychic readings. Comic Con fans will enjoy this event, too, since it celebrates cosplay, nerd culture, sci-fi, fantasy, horror, and more.

119 E. Bridge St., Granbury
817-559-0849
granburyparanormalexpo.com

YUCK IT UP
WITH FOUR DAY WEEKEND'S
UNIQUE COMEDY IMPROV

Although they've been performing every Friday and Saturday night since 1997, no two Four Day Weekend performances are alike. Over the years, this Fort Worth–based comedy troupe has developed a unique style of improv. Before each show, audience members are encouraged to write random sentences on index cards and Post-it notes. Throughout the nearly two-hour performance, cast members use these phrases to create hilarious improvisational scenes. A few audience members will be drawn into the performance, too, but it's all good fun. Although the nightclub is eighteen and older and may include adult themes, the humor is not overtly "blue," and Four Day Weekend prides itself on being a class act. As of this writing, they have also expanded to a second location in Dallas.

312 Houston St., Fort Worth
817-226-4329
fourdayweekend.com

OTHER PLACES TO CATCH SOME LAUGHS:

Hyena's
Fort Worth, Dallas, Plano
817-877-5233
hyenascomedynightclub.com

Addison Improv
4980 Belt Line Rd., Ste. 250, Dallas
866-468-3399
improvaddison.com

Dallas Comedy House
3025 Main St., Dallas
214-741-4448
dallascomedyhouse.com

CZECH OUT
THE NATIONAL POLKA FESTIVAL IN ENNIS

For more than fifty years, accordion music and the smell of fresh-baked kolaches have wafted through the air for three days each May as citizens of Czech and Slavic heritage celebrated the National Polka Festival in Ennis. Most of the festivities center around the historic downtown area with parades, beer tents, arts and crafts vendors, carnival rides, dancing, and, of course, live polka bands! This family-friendly event also includes costumed dancers, a kolache eating contest, a flag ceremony, face painting, a rock climbing wall, and bounce houses. Food vendors offer classic festival foods, such as funnel cakes and corn dogs, as well as traditional Czech goodies, such as klobase. The city provides free shuttles to make parking for this busy event easier.

200 NW Main St., Ennis
972-878-4748
nationalpolkafestival.com

EXPLORE DEEP ELLUM
FOR ECLECTIC AND ARTSY BIG D FUN

With its eclectic mix of funky coffee shops, restaurants, art galleries, and public murals, Deep Ellum is a fun place to visit day or night. This artsy Dallas neighborhood has roots dating back to 1873 when it became one of the first business centers for European immigrants and African-Americans. Although Henry Ford once manufactured Model Ts here, music is what really put Deep Ellum on the map. In the 1920s, the area became a hub for rising jazz and blues performers. Today, Deep Ellum boasts more than sixty restaurants, thirty shops, and more than twenty live music venues. Be sure to drop by the biweekly flea market and add the annual Deep Ellum Arts Festival to your calendar.

Overview of Deep Ellum (full list of venues):
deepellumtexas.com

Deep Ellum Outdoor Market
100-199 N. Crowdus St., Dallas
facebook.com/deepellummarket

Deep Ellum Arts Festival
2900-3400 Main St., Dallas
214-855-1881
deepellumartsfestival.com

SIDLE UP TO THE WHITE ELEPHANT SALOON
FOR HISTORIC WESTERN FLAVOR

If you want to feel like you've walked onto the set of a Western movie, consider dropping by the White Elephant Saloon. This historic watering hole is notorious for being the site of Fort Worth's final Wild West-era gunfight, which played out between Longhair Jim Courtright and White Elephant Saloon owner Luke Short. History buffs and Western fans will enjoy the annual costumed reenactment, and children are welcome to attend. For additional Western flavor, grab a bowl of Texas-style chili with a side of cornbread while you're here. The walls are lined with cowboy hats and, as you might expect, an assortment of white elephants. There's a small dance floor, and the live music featured nightly is heavy on country and western.

106 E. Exchange Ave., Fort Worth
817-624-8273
whiteelephantsaloon.com

SEE WHAT'S HAPPENING
IN THE DALLAS ARTS DISTRICT

The Dallas Arts District is America's largest art district. This cluster of nineteen city blocks is spread over sixty-eight acres and jam-packed with performance halls, museums, and public art. Museums here include the Nasher Sculpture Center, Dallas Museum of Art, and the Crow Collection of Asian Art. Live performance venues include the Meyerson Symphony Center, the Winspear Opera House, and the Wyly Theatre.

Throughout the year, the Dallas Arts District hosts block parties featuring pop-up performances from local artists, social media scavenger hunts, food trucks, and family-friendly fun. Keep an eye on their website for details to all the events here, or just drop by for a stroll through Klyde Warren Park and see what's going on today.

Dallas Arts District
214-744-6642
dallasartsdistrict.org

STUDY TEXAS HISTORY,
WITH A SIDE OF GHOSTS

As Shelly Tucker likes to say, "Sometimes folks come to Denton and never want to leave, ever!" Shelly, or the "ghost lady" as she is known around town, leads the wildly popular Ghosts of Denton Haunted History Tour. A few years ago the National Endowment for the Arts (NEA) acknowledged Shelly's storytelling prowess by naming her an "American Masterpiece." Not everyone considers themselves a "history buff," but when you wrap a good ghost story around true local lore, you get the best of both worlds. Shelly's tour is just one of several haunted history tours offered throughout the DFW Metroplex.

Ghosts of Denton Haunted History Tour
Jupiter House, 106 N. Locust St., Denton
817-996-9775
ghostsofdenton.com

OTHER GHOST TOURS:

Burleson Historical Ghost Tour
124 W. Ellison St., Burleson
817-889-1610
burlesonhistoricalghosttour.
com

Fort Worth Ghost Tours
(Varies; several different tours available)
817-501-1086
fortworthghosts.com

Fort Worth Stockyard Ghost Tour
112 W. Exchange Ave.
Fort Worth
817-626-1011
stockyardsghosttour.com

Goatman's Bridge Tour
Old Alton Bridge, Argyle
becksghosthunters.com

Granbury Ghosts & Legends Tour
817-559-0849
119 E. Bridge St., Granbury
granburytours.com

Grapevine Night Watchman Ghost Tour
409 S. Main St., Grapevine
817-329-1011
grapevinespringswinery.
com/new-index-1/#ghost-tours

Lewisville: Gateway Ghost Tours
208 E. Main St., Lewisville
972-922-4675
gatewayghosttours.com

McKinney History, Ghosts & Legends Walking Tour
300 E. Virginia St.
McKinney
facebook.com/pg/
texpartparanormal/events

Mineral Wells: Baker Hotel Ghost Walk
200 E. Hubbard St.
Mineral Wells
817-629-8127
facebook.com/pg/
thebakerhotelghostwalk

Terrell Ghost Walk
106 E. Moore Ave., Terrell
972-546-7536

WALK THE RED CARPET
AT THE MODERN'S ANNUAL OSCAR WATCHING PARTY

Every year the Modern Art Museum of Fort Worth hosts an Oscar Watching Party. This free event is much better than sitting at home watching the gala event on TV. Why should West Coast VIPs have all the fun? Papparazzi and journalists greet visitors at the entrance and snap red carpet photos of every single "celebrity" who walks through the door, including you. You can watch the Academy Awards in the auditorium, but the people-watching is truly top notch. Not only will you see snappy tuxedos and glittering gowns galore, but many people also dress as their favorite movie characters, past and present. During commercial breaks, the emcees even give out prizes. An open bar, snacks, and a slew of generous prizes round out the offerings.

3200 Darnell St., Fort Worth
817-738-9215
themodern.org

SWING INTO SPRING
AT THE ANNUAL JAZZ AGE
SUNDAY SOCIAL

Each spring the Art Deco Society of Dallas hosts a Jazz Age Sunday Social at Dallas Heritage Village. The living history park makes the perfect backdrop for this vintage-inspired event, which includes an antique automobile show, classic games (e.g., horseshoes and badminton), vendors, ice cream, live jazz music, and a photo booth. Participants are encouraged to dress the part, so don your snazziest whites or other 1920s era garb. The best dressed Dappers and Flappers will win a prize, and volunteers are on hand to teach you how to cut a rug. That said period attire is not required. Either way pack your picnic lunch and prepare to enjoy. Whether you take to the dance floor or simply kick back and enjoy the tunes, this annual event is truly the bee's knees.

Dallas Heritage Village at Old City Park
1515 S. Harwood St., Dallas
jazzagesundaysocial.com

SPORTS AND RECREATION

PLAY "KOI"
AT THE FORT WORTH BOTANIC GARDEN'S JAPANESE GARDEN

Not only is the Fort Worth Botanic Garden on the National Register of Historic Places, but it is also the oldest botanic garden in Texas, having been established in 1934. With twenty-three specialty gardens spread over 109 acres, you can easily spend a day here. The grounds include a European-style rose garden, a 10,000-square-foot conservatory filled with tropical plants, and a section dedicated to native plants. The seven-acre Japanese garden is a definite highlight with its koi-filled ponds, pagodas, teahouse, waterfalls, and beautifully manicured cherry trees. If you work up an appetite, enjoy a meal at The Gardens restaurant. Two charming gift shops are also on-site.

3220 Botanic Garden Blvd., Fort Worth
817-392-5510
fwbg.org

TAKE A
NORTH TEXAS SAFARI
AT FOSSIL RIM WILDLIFE CENTER

Fossil Rim Wildlife Center is a safari park with more than a thousand African and Asian animals roaming the grounds. A trip here offers the thrill of seeing exotic animals up close. In fact, the animals are used to humans and will approach your vehicle hoping for snacks. (You can get a bag of animal feed when you buy your tickets.) If you don't want to use your vehicle, the park provides a wide range of guided tours. You can even stay the night at Fossil Rim's on-site lodge. If you visit during the summer months, get to the park early since many animals retreat to the shade during midday. There is a reasonably priced café halfway through, but remember to bring water so that you won't be rushed.

2299 County Road 2008, Glen Rose
254-897-2960
fossilrim.org

SEE WHAT'S BLOOMING
AT THE DALLAS ARBORETUM

The Dallas Arboretum spans sixty-six acres along White Rock Lake. A series of pathways link twelve distinctly different gardens throughout this well-groomed park, and something is always blooming. The gardens only close three days each year: Thanksgiving, Christmas Day, and New Year's Day. Picnicking is encouraged, but two restaurants are located on the grounds. Be sure to take a free tour of the DeGolyer Mansion. This 21,000-square-foot dwelling was once the home of a wealthy geologist and his wife. Of its many colorful seasonal events, the annual Pumpkin Patch Village is not to be missed. The park offers free trams and wheelchairs on a first-come, first-served basis. Wagons for toting children (and picnic items) are available for a small rental fee.

8525 Garland Rd., Dallas
214-515-6615
dallasarboretum.org

STROLL THROUGH THE LIVING ART
OF CHANDOR GARDENS

From 1936 until 1952, the internationally renowned portrait artist Douglas Chandor and his wife transformed their Weatherford estate into a lush garden compound. He considered the result "living art," and his wife dubbed it "Chandor Gardens." The landscaping is a blend of English-style gardens, with Asian influences, such as a koi pond and a bronze sea dragon fountain. In places, it really feels as if you are walking through a painting. At a mere four acres, Chandor Gardens is a different experience than the sixty-six-acre Dallas Arboretum or the 109-acre Fort Worth Botanic Gardens, but that's part of its charm. Even in Texas, bigger isn't always better. The city of Weatherford now operates this enchanting space, which is both open to the public and available for private functions.

711 W. Lee Ave,, Weatherford
817-613-1700
chandorgardens.mynewsarchive.com

REEL IN CATFISH AND TROUT
FOR FREE AT DFW'S STOCKED PONDS

The Texas Parks and Wildlife Department stocks ponds throughout the DFW Metroplex every two to four weeks throughout the year. From April through November, catfish are stocked in most lakes. (Due to the extreme Texas heat, fish are not stocked in August.) Since they prefer cooler temperatures, rainbow trout are stocked from late November through March. It all adds up to year-round fishing fun with friends and family at such lakes as the ones listed below. Don't worry if you lack fishing equipment. The Tackle Loaner Program lets you borrow what you need for free.

Tackle Loaner Program:
tpwd.texas.gov/education/angler-education/tackle-loaner-program

Dallas-Fort Worth Fisheries on Facebook
817-732-0761
facebook.com/tpwdifftworth

FIVE STOCKED PONDS TO TRY:

South Lakes Park Pond
556 Hobson Ln., Denton

Chisholm Park
2200 Norwood Dr., Hurst

Greenbriar Park
5200 Hemphill St., Fort Worth

Lakeside Park
515 Hill City Dr., Duncanville

City Lake Park
200 Parkview Ln., Mesquite

TRAIPSE THROUGH TREETOPS
AT THE DALLAS WORLD AQUARIUM

Don't let the name fool you. The Dallas World Aquarium is more than just a fun place to see fancy fish. Even the nondescript exterior of this former warehouse belies the lush interior inside. Yes, there are aquariums, but the space is more like a giant South American terrarium, which includes birds, jaguars, tropical plants, and even penguins. Walkways allow you to meander through treetops, where exotic birds fly through the branches, completely uncaged. Footpaths continue to the ground level and even below, where you can watch manatees, waterfowl, and fish swim around a forty-foot waterfall. The plants are amazing too. You don't even need to leave for lunch; the venue includes three restaurants. They even serve beer and ice-cold margaritas. What's not to love?

1801 N. Griffin St., Dallas
214-720-2224
dwazoo.com

FLOAT AND WATCH WATERFRONT CONCERTS
AT PANTHER ISLAND PAVILION

Panther Island Pavilion is a unique entertainment venue situated along the Trinity River, with Fort Worth's city skyline as a backdrop. Events here include concerts, festivals, runs, and more. Panther Island Pavilion features the only waterfront stage in Texas, so concertgoers can float in the water as they listen to live performances. You don't even need to have your own gear. Kayaks, canoes, and paddleboards are available for rental on-site. Even when there are no special events, locals have been coming here for years to cool off during the summer. There's free public access to the Trinity River to swim, kayak, tube, and fish.

395 Purcey St., Fort Worth
817-698-0700
pantherislandpavilion.com

DELIGHT IN OLD-FASHIONED SWIMMING HOLE FUN
AT BURGER'S LAKE

When I asked for suggestions to include on this list of one hundred things, readers beseeched me to include Burger's Lake. This privately owned and operated venue in Fort Worth includes a spring-fed lake, picnic areas (with grills), rope swings, slides, diving boards, and two beach areas with lifeguards on duty. Aside from providing a respite from hot Texas summers, Burger's Lake offers a slice of yesteryear in the form of an old-style swimming hole. Even with all the kids running around, it's much quieter and relaxing than a modern-day waterpark. Burger's Lake is the type of place you bring the whole family to create lasting memories.

1200 Meandering Rd., Fort Worth
817-737-3414
burgerslake.com

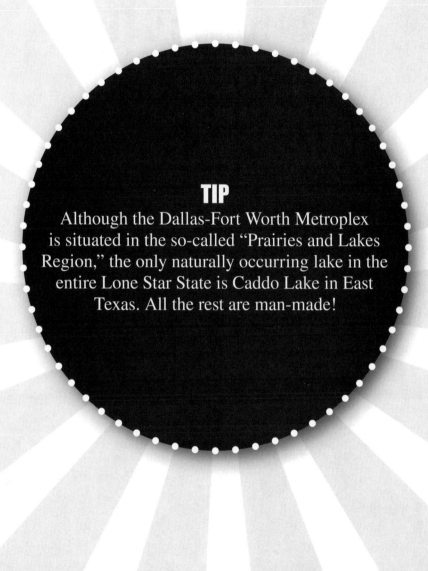

TIP

Although the Dallas-Fort Worth Metroplex is situated in the so-called "Prairies and Lakes Region," the only naturally occurring lake in the entire Lone Star State is Caddo Lake in East Texas. All the rest are man-made!

LEARN HOW TO FISH
AT THE TEXAS FRESHWATER FISHERIES CENTER

The Texas Freshwater Fisheries Center (TFFC) is a full-production freshwater fish hatchery dedicated to the preservation of Texas wetlands. Visitors can enjoy three hundred thousand gallons of freshwater fish exhibits, featuring catfish, gar, bass, alligators, and more. There's also a freshwater dive show followed by a free tram tour of the freshwater fish production facility. Afterward, stretch your legs on the paved wetland trail, which offers educational exhibits along the way. Best of all, if you'd like to go fishing, the TFFC staff will not only let you borrow a rod, reel, and bait, but they'll also give you a free fishing lesson. Who knows? Afterward, fresh fish may be on your home menu!

5550 FM 2495, Athens
903-676-2277
tpwd.texas.gov/spdest/visitorcenters/tffc

ADMIRE
THE CRAFTSMANSHIP
AT WOOD, WAVES, AND WHEELS

If you enjoy classic boats, cars, and motorcycles, don't miss Wood, Waves, and Wheels. Each May the Fort Worth Boat Club hosts this show at its elegant lakeside venue in conjunction with the Eagle Mountain Classic Boat Club. Classic cars and bikes are displayed on the lawn, while vintage boats float in the marina. Attendees may vote for their favorite vehicles, with prizes given for People's Choice, Judge's Favorites, and Best of Show. There's even a costume contest for the best vintage boating outfit. Weather permitting, there's often a boat show to cap off the day. Wood, Waves, and Wheels is free to the public, with refreshments available for purchase. Parking is also free, but the lot fills quickly, so get there early.

1000 Boat Club Rd., Fort Worth
facebook.com/pg/eaglemountainclassicboatclub

TAKE TIME TO SMELL THE FLOWERS
ON THE ENNIS BLUEBONNET TRAILS

While these colorful lupines bloom throughout the Lone Star State each spring, in 1997 the State Legislature dubbed Ennis the "Official Bluebonnet City of Texas." The convention and visitors bureau and local garden club take this honor so seriously that they devote the entire month of April to keeping tabs of the blossoms. To this end, more than forty miles have been mapped and designated as the Ennis Bluebonnet Trails. The Ennis CVB is open seven days a week, so visitors are encouraged to plan ahead by calling for an update, visiting their website, or downloading the Ennis Y'all free mobile app for iPhone and Android. The app includes a full directory of events, attractions, accommodations, restaurants, shops, and more, as well as a bluebonnet trail map with GPS locations.

204 W. Knox St., Ennis
972-878-4748
visitennis.org/bluebonnet.htm

MARVEL AT RODEO RIDING AND ROPING SKILLS
IN FORT WORTH AND MESQUITE

Rodeo is a competitive sport based on the riding and roping skills American cowboys needed for survival. Considering the historic impact cattle drives had upon the DFW Metroplex, consider checking out a rodeo while you are here. April through September is rodeo season, and each year during this time the Resistol Arena hosts the Mesquite Rodeo. The original rodeo venue began in 1958 as a rugged outdoor affair, a far cry from the modern air-conditioned arena that exists today and has played host to the likes of President Ronald Reagan, President George W. Bush, and Prince Rainier III of Monaco. For year-round rodeo entertainment, check out the Stockyards Championship Rodeo, which offers rodeo competitions every single weekend in Fort Worth.

Mesquite Rodeo
1818 Rodeo Dr., Mesquite
972-285-8777
mesquiterodeo.com

Stockyards Championship Rodeo
121 E. Exchange Ave., Fort Worth
817-625-1025
stockyardsrodeo.com

TAKE TO THE SKIES
IN CAVANAUGH FLIGHT MUSEUM'S HISTORIC WAR BIRDS

Tucked beside Dallas Love Field, the Frontiers of Flight Museum is a boldly designed 100,000-square-foot hangar-style building. Exhibits here take you through the history of flight, from general aviation to military aircraft, beginning with Leonard Da Vinci's parachute designs and continuing straight up to modern space vehicles. In addition to exhibits, the facility includes more than thirty aircraft, a 200-seat auditorium, classrooms, conference rooms, a gift shop, and free parking. History buffs will especially enjoy the Cavanaugh Flight Museum, which has an extensive collection of vintage military aircraft. Many of these "War Birds" are in such good condition that you can actually book scenic tours in them. This museum is a nonprofit organization dedicated to aviation history.

Frontiers of Flight Museum
6911 Lemmon Ave., Dallas
214-350-3600
flightmuseum.com

Cavanaugh Flight Museum
4572 Claire Chennault St., Addison
972-380-8800
cavflight.org

REFRESH YOURSELF
AT THE FORT WORTH WATER GARDENS

The Fort Worth Water Gardens are a modern take on ancient city fountains, with Mother Nature as the theme instead of cherubs and Roman gods. Built in 1974 by prestigious architects Philip Johnson and John Burgee, this park covers 4.3 acres smack dab in the middle of downtown Fort Worth. Even though flanked by skyscrapers and Interstate 30, the Water Gardens successfully creates a contemplative oasis in the middle of a busy urban environment. Best of all, this peaceful space is free to the public and open every single day. The park is divided into four unique spaces: the Active Pool, the Aerating Pool, the Quiet Pool, and the Mountain. If the Active Pool looks familiar to you, you may recognize it from the 1975 sci-fi movie *Logan's Run*.

1502 Commerce St., Fort Worth
817-392-7111
fortworth.com/things-to-do/attractions/fort-worth-water-gardens

BEAT THE HEAT
AT THE GALLERIA ICE RINK

Here in North Texas snow is a rarity, and our lakes never freeze over. So even if you don't enter the rink, watching people skate in the middle of a busy Dallas mall is quite a sight, especially during the Christmas season, when a huge and festively decorated pine tree stands in the middle of the ice. Over the years, several Olympic skating champs have taken a spin on the Galleria Dallas ice rink, but for most folks in the DFW Metroplex, it's just a great way to beat the heat and let you and your kids burn off some excess energy. No need to bring your own gear. The Galleria offers skate rentals and lessons.

13350 Dallas Pkwy., Ste. 200, Dallas
972-392-3363
galleriaiceskatingcenter.com

ENJOY NORTH TEXAS HILL COUNTRY
AT CEDAR HILL STATE PARK

Nicknamed the "hill country of Dallas," Cedar Hill is a great place to escape the hectic pace of the city. After perusing the shops and photo ops in its historic town square, venture to Cedar Hill State Park for a healthy dose of Mother Nature. The park sits along the edge of Joe Pool Lake and includes more than eighteen hundred acres of rolling hills and woods. There are campsites, picnic areas, hiking trails, playgrounds, geocaching, places to fish, and a gravel swimming beach to keep your whole family entertained. You could even just kick back and read a book in the shade, but make sure you bring binoculars. The park is full of wildlife, including bobcats, armadillos, and coyotes.

Historic Downtown Cedar Hill
600 Cedar St., Cedar Hill
972-291-5100
cedarhilltx.com/90/historic-downtown

Cedar Hill State Park
1570 W. FM 1382, Cedar Hill
972-291-3900
cedarhillstatepark.org

CULTURE AND HISTORY

PLAY HIDE-AND-SEEK WITH DINOSAURS
AT THE FORT WORTH MUSEUM OF SCIENCE AND HISTORY

The Fort Worth Museum of Science and History started off as a children's museum and continues to offer plenty of hands-on exhibits geared toward children, especially in the Innovation Studio area, where visitors of all ages are encouraged to learn scientific principles through interactive play. The archaeology section replicates an actual dig site and features full-scale skeletons of the towering creatures that once roamed North Texas, while an interactive motion screen lets visitors play hide-and-seek from hungry raptors. Admission includes star shows at the Noble Planetarium and the on-site Cattle Raisers museum. You'll have to pay extra to view shows in the Omni Theater, which is the the biggest IMAX dome west of the Mississippi. This movie-watching dome is eight stories high and uses a 120-foot-wide screen to take viewers on immersive journeys.

1600 Gendy St., Fort Worth
817-255-9300
fwmuseum.org

WALK THROUGH 1313 MOCKINGBIRD LANE
DURING THE MUNSTER MANSION OPEN HOUSE

While you can't set your GPS for "1313 Mockingbird Lane," you can visit an incredible replica of the Munster family home in the town of Waxahachie. In 2001, Sandra and Charles McKee built a replica of the creepy home depicted in the 1960s-era TV sitcom. The pair carefully rewatched all seventy episodes of The Munsters to perfect their design, which includes a fire-breathing creature under the staircase.

Despite the effort the McKees put into creating their Munster Mansion, it is not a year-round tourist attraction. For them, it is simply a fun project. Even so, since 2002, the McKees have sponsored a two-day Munster Mansion Open House each fall. All proceeds go to local charities. To find out when the next open house will be, visit the official Munster Mansion website.

Exact address withheld out of courtesy to the McKees. To attend the next Munster Mansion Open House, watch for details at the official website: munstermansion.com

ADMIRE DA VINCI'S "WAX SUPPER"
AT THE CHRISTIAN ARTS MUSEUM

In 1955, oil tycoon Bill Fleming commissioned a version of Leonardo Da Vinci's masterpiece *The Last Supper*. Instead of a painting, however, Fleming paid for a life-sized sculpture made from wax. To complete this project, Fleming hired the mother/daughter team of Katherine and Katherine Marie Stubergh, a duo well known for their wax sculptures. After eighteen months, their "Wax Supper" was done, and Bill Fleming gave it to the city of Fort Worth. For the next forty years, the waxwork made the rounds from churches to a shopping mall. In 1997, it was placed in storage, and for a while all seemed lost. In 2009, however, the wax display was restored. The Stubergh's "Wax Supper" is currently on display at the Christian Arts Museum in Fort Worth, where entry is free of charge.

3221 Hamilton Ave., Fort Worth
817-332-7878
facebook.com/ChristianArtsMuseumFW

STOMP FRESH FRUIT
IN YOUR BARE FEET DURING GRAPEFEST
IN GRAPEVINE

Did you know that Texas was home to the first vineyard in North America? It's no wonder then that the city of Grapevine hosts the largest wine festival in the Southwest. Called "GrapeFest," this four-day extravaganza features live music, artwork, handmade jewelry, carnival rides, and wine tasting galore. Wine-related events include the People's Choice Wine Tasting Classic, the Texas Wine Tribute, a GrapeStomp, and the Champagne Cork Shoot-Off. GrapeFest uses a coupon system instead of cash for buying food, drinks, and rides. Bargain hunters will appreciate that Thursday's admission is always free. Check the festival website to find out about free off-site parking with complimentary shuttle rides.

One Liberty Park Plaza, Grapevine
800-457-6338
grapevinetexasusa.com

ESCAPE INTO THE PAST
AT THE DALLAS HERITAGE VILLAGE

If you've ever wanted to escape from the stress of modern life and step into the past, then head over to Dallas Heritage Village in Old City Park. More than thirty historic buildings from 1840 to 1910 were painstakingly moved and reassembled to create a living history museum. Today, the twenty-acre village includes a bank, print shop, blacksmith, Greek Revival schoolhouse, store, hotel, saloon, law office, and more. This historic time capsule is staffed by docents in period garb who give tours and demonstrate old-time activities, such as blacksmithing, wood shopping, wool spinning, and candlemaking. The village offers special tours for children and adults, and the annual Candlelight Celebration offers a taste of Victorian Era Christmas traditions, including carolers, donkey-pulled carriages, baked goods, and holiday crafts.

1515 S. Harwood St., Dallas
214-413-3679
dallasheritagevillage.org

HOLD SNAKES AND FEED PARAKEETS
AT THE FORT WORTH ZOO

The Fort Worth Zoo has come a long way since it first opened in 1909. Back then it only housed a handful of exotic species. These days it consistently ranks among the top ten zoos in America. This animal park caters to all ages. Between the petting zoo, aviary, and the reptile house (aka "Museum of Living Art" or MOLA), visitors have many opportunities for hands-on interaction with animals. Shady paths are much appreciated on a hot summer day, and a $3 tram is available if you or the little ones poop out. The grounds are dotted with food options, ranging from sit-down cafés to snack shacks. Keep an eye on the event calendar because the zoo offers special events throughout the year, including overnight stays complete with dinner and a scavenger hunt.

1989 Colonial Pkwy., Fort Worth
817-759-7555
fortworthzoo.org

WALK THE GARDEN LABYRINTH
AT THE NATIONAL VIETNAM WAR MUSEUM

As you drive by, the Vietnam-era Huey helicopter mounted in the air is likely to be the first thing you notice here. Overall, the National Vietnam War Museum is not your typical museum featuring indoor exhibits in glass cases. Instead, it offers a series of outdoor monuments, gardens, and displays connected by wheelchair/stroller-friendly pebble pathways. The Meditation Garden showcases two garden labyrinths winding through a variety of plants tended by the local Parker County Master Gardeners. The Vietnam Memorial Garden section features a 300-foot-long half-scale replica of the Vietnam Memorial in Washington, DC. The names inscribed upon it are updated annually. A computer kiosk on-site helps visitors find specific names on the wall, and there is a Visitor Center, too, if you have any questions.

12685 Mineral Wells Hwy. (US Hwy. 180), Weatherford
940-325-4003
nationalvnwarmuseum.org

BATHE IN CRAZY WATER
AT THE FAMOUS WATER COMPANY

In 1904, a pharmacist, who claimed drinking the water of Mineral Wells cured him of a fatal illness, opened the Famous Water Company so that he could sell the miraculous fluid. Nicknamed "crazy water" by locals, this local mineral water continues to sell throughout the DFW Metroplex. In fact, if you visit the Famous Water Company's shop, you can even bathe in it.

Built in the 1920s, the Baker Hotel was the first skyscraper erected outside a major metropolitan area, and it still looms large over the small town of Mineral Wells. In its glory, the Baker catered to the likes of Will Rogers, Helen Keller, Judy Garland, and Bonnie and Clyde. Although currently closed to the public, it's worth stopping by and snapping photos of this eye-catching landmark.

Famous Water Company
209 NW Sixth St., Mineral Wells
940-325-8870
drinkcrazywater.com

Baker Hotel
200 E. Hubbard St., Mineral Wells
940-325-2557
thebakerhotel.com

FIND FOSSILIZED FOOTPRINTS
AT DINOSAUR VALLEY STATE PARK

This being Texas, our state dinosaur isn't just big. It is arguably the largest creature to have ever walked the earth. Another great thing about our dino is that you don't have to visit a museum to see evidence of its existence. Much like the famous movie star handprints in front of Grauman's Chinese Theatre in Los Angeles, Pauluxysaurus Jonesi left footprints all over Glen Rose and its surroundings. A great place to see them is at Dinosaur Valley State Park, where the Pauluxy River's claylike mud perfectly preserves several of the huge creature's footprints. When the river is low, these ancient footprints are easy to see. If the river is up, you may have to get your feet wet, but it's definitely worth it.

629 Park Road 59, Glen Rose
254-897-4588
tpwd.state.tx.us/state-parks/dinosaur-valley

GET THE SCOOP
ON DALLAS
AT THE OLD RED MUSEUM

If you have driven through downtown Dallas, chances are you have noticed the Old Red Museum. With its turrets, gargoyles, archways, and beautiful red sandstone brickwork, it is an eye-catching building and delightfully old-fashioned beside all the modern skyscrapers that flank it. Whether you are interested in politics, business, archaeology, or those intriguing little details that made life so different in the past, the Old Red Museum has something to interest you. This museum chronicles regional history from ancient times right up to the present day, offering something for all age levels and attention spans. Visitors can learn about everything from the ancient mammoth to the notorious Bonnie and Clyde through touch screen monitors, four theaters, and five separate display rooms.

100 S. Houston St., Dallas
214-745-1100
oldred.org

EXPERIENCE PIONEER LIFE
AT LOG CABIN VILLAGE

Log Cabin Village is a living history museum made up of nine historic log cabins dating from the mid to late 1800s. Visitors will enjoy a mixture of hands-on activities along with demonstrations of the skills it took for pioneers to live from day to day, such as spinning wool, grinding corn, candlemaking, and forging iron. Costumed historical interpreters do a great job imparting their knowledge and passion for history. Bring a picnic basket with and savor the parklike setting before making the rounds. Take time to sit near the herb garden or the waterwheel and just imagine what life was like here more than a century ago. Keep an eye on their event calendar to catch such events as "Folk Songs of the Cowboy & Pioneer" and "Cherokee Basket Weaving" throughout the year.

2100 Log Cabin Village Ln., Fort Worth
817-392-5881
logcabinvillage.org

REFLECT ON VICTORIAN ERA LIFE
AT THE TEXAS CIVIL WAR MUSEUM

You don't need to be a devout history buff to enjoy a trip to the Texas Civil War Museum. A short film loops at the front of the building, providing enough context for anyone to enjoy the exhibits. The museum is thoughtfully laid out. Union items line the north wall, and Confederate items line the south. While many of the artifacts relate directly to battle (e.g., guns and knives), other aspects of the Civil War are represented here, too, such as soldiers' sewing kits, musical instruments, and the equipment used to perform amputations. A large section is also devoted to Victorian dresses and gowns. If you have children with you, the museum provides activity sheets to help them enjoy the museum while learning something new.

760 Jim Wright Freeway N., Fort Worth
817-246-2323
texascivilwarmuseum.com

WATCH THE CITY'S LONGHORN HERD STRUT ITS STUFF
AT THE FORT WORTH STOCKYARDS DAILY CATTLE DRIVES

Fort Worth's famous livestock market may be gone, but the cattle drive lives on. Twice a day Cowtown's official city herd of longhorn cows saunters down East Exchange Avenue.These steers were bred for walking all day long, so a short jaunt down the street takes only a few minutes. If you miss their outing, you can still visit them in their corral. While there keep an eye out for cattle drovers dressed in nineteenth century garb, who are happy to pose for pictures with you and answer questions about life in the Old West.

131 E. Exchange Ave., Fort Worth
800-433-5747
fortworth.com/the-herd

CHECK OUT CLEBURNE'S
CARNEGIE LIBRARY AND
RAILROAD MUSEUM

Cleburne's Layland Museum is housed in a historic Carnegie Library building. Architecture buffs will enjoy the building as much as the exhibits about early settlers inside, since the stately Greek Revival building features Ionic columns, ornate decorative plasterwork, and original furnishings throughout.

Next door you'll find the Cleburne Railroad Museum, where photos, historic items, and displays illustrate the impact that the arrival (and departure) of the Santa Fe Railroad had upon small towns, such as Cleburne. A short movie at the front of the museum gives a good overview of the exhibits. Railroad fans of all ages will love the model train on display, while school-age children can become "Junior Conductors" by taking the Time Table Challenge, a free worksheet provided by the museum.

Layland Museum
201 N. Caddo St., Cleburne
871-645-0940
laylandmuseum.com

Cleburne Railroad Museum
206 N. Main St., Cleburne
817-645-0952
cleburne.net/1051/cleburne-railroad-museum

● ●

WATCH HISTORY COME TO LIFE
AT THE OAKWOOD CEMETERY
SAINTS & SINNERS TOUR

What do you get when you combine live theater, regional history, and a beautiful Texas graveyard? Why, the Annual Oakwood Cemetery Saints & Sinners Tour, of course! Each fall members of the North Fort Worth Historical Society choose notable figures from Oakwood Cemetery's residents to "bring to life" through well-researched performances spaced throughout the grounds. The monologues are often a bit humorous, although some will bring tears to your eyes. The walking tour itself lasts about one and a half hours (depending on which of the three tour guides you go with), and you can easily spend another hour or two chatting with the historic reenactors, listening to the live bluegrass music, and exploring the beautiful grounds. This unique tour brings history alive in a very moving and often humorous way.

701 Grand Ave., Fort Worth
stockyardsmuseum.org/historical-society-meeting---special-events.html

WATCH MILLIONS IN THE MAKING
AT THE BUREAU OF ENGRAVING AND PRINTING

The buck stops here! Or perhaps it starts here, since the Bureau of Engraving and Printing cranks out cash by the ream at this factory. Over half of the paper money in America is printed here. In fact, if you look in your wallet and see any paper bills with a tiny "FW" printed on them, they were printed at this Fort Worth facility. This is a government operation with tight security, so leave your cell phone, digital camera, and any other electronic gizmos locked up in your car. After watching a short film, you can take the self-guided tour. The moneymaking process is intricate and surprisingly mesmerizing. Ironically perhaps, tours here are free. Remember your wallet, however, because the gift shop is full of interesting souvenirs.

9000 Blue Mound Rd., Fort Worth
817-231-4000
moneyfactory.gov/fortworthtxtours.html

ENJOY COLORFUL SKIES
DURING THE PLANO BALLOON FESTIVAL

For more than thirty years, brightly colored hot-air balloons have taken to the skies every September during the Plano Balloon Festival. This three-day-long event is Plano's largest annual celebration, bringing some ninety thousand attendees per year! Festivities are centered in Oak Point Park and include concerts, fireworks, skydivers, crafts, food vendors, arts and crafts sellers, and a Kids Fun Zone. While the balloons make a colorful sight by day, try to attend a nighttime balloon glow event, which is when balloon pilots create a synchronized display using their balloons' burners. Since this is an outdoor event, some aspects depend on the weather, so some activities may be canceled or postponed. Come see why Plano is known as the Hot Air Balloon Capital of Texas.

2801 E. Spring Creek Pkwy., Plano
972-867-7566
planoballoonfest.org

VISIT THE HISTORIC MARKER
FOR A SPACE ALIEN'S GRAVE
IN AURORA CEMETERY

In April 1897, the *Dallas News* reported a UFO crash in the Wise County town of Aurora. According to the reporter, although the petite alien was "not an inhabitant of this world," his or her body was buried in the local cemetery. This bizarre legend remains popular among mystery seekers and is even mentioned on a Texas State Historical Marker at the site. In recent years, the city of Aurora has embraced its strange legacy by hosting an Aurora Alien Expo, incorporating a bug-eyed alien into the city logo and even erecting a sculpture of a crashed spaceship as you enter town. Keep an eye on the city's website for tours of the crash site and grave as well as alien-themed festivals throughout the year.

507 Cemetery Rd., Aurora
auroratexas.gov

LEARN COWBOY CULTURE
AT THESE FORT WORTH MUSEUMS

While a trip to the historic Stockyards District offers a taste of why Fort Worth is known as "where the West begins," the following museums offer more insights into cowboy culture. The Amon Carter Museum of American Art showcases renowned Western artists Remington and Russell, while the Cattle Raisers Museum (located inside the Fort Worth Museum of Science and History) features exhibits about the nitty-gritty realities of ranch life. Lest we forget that women were a big part of how the West was won, a visit to the National Cowgirl Museum and Hall of Fame offers a glimpse into the often overlooked contributions made by America's cowgirls.

Amon Carter Museum of American Art
3501 Camp Bowie Blvd., Fort Worth
cartermuseum.org

Cattle Raisers Museum
1600 Gendy St., Fort Worth
817-332-8551
cattleraisersmuseum.org

National Cowgirl Museum and Hall of Fame
1720 Gendy St., Fort Worth
817-336-4475
cowgirl.net

ADMIRE THOUSANDS OF HISTORIC FIGURINES
AT THE GRANBURY DOLL HOUSE

Founded in 2012 by sisters Jane Sharp and Barbara Williams, the Granbury Doll House displays more than twenty-five hundred dolls from around the world throughout a two-story historic home. Collectors who donate their treasures to this unique museum are reassured that their dolls will be treated with loving care and displayed for others to enjoy. The exhibits are arranged chronologically, starting with handmade dolls from early settlers. As you proceed through the house, you will see everything from mass-produced Barbies and G.I. Joes to handcrafted one-of-a-kind pieces from famous dollmakers. One of the most unique exhibits is a 1922 Dolly Rekord doll. It contains a wax cylinder created by Thomas Edison that allows it to "speak." Admission is free, and if the American flag is out, the museum is open.

421 E. Bridge St., Granbury
817-894-5194
facebook.com/thegranburydollhouse

RIDE THE RAILS
ON THE GRAPEVINE VINTAGE RAILROAD

The Grapevine Vintage Railroad (GVVR) features six coaches that can carry up to 394 passengers. Some of these Victorian Era train cars have beautiful mahogany bars for beverage service. All are heated in cold weather, but first-class passengers can also enjoy air-conditioning. The GVVR offers a variety of excursions. Some return you to your starting point, so you can catch the train from Grapevine and return to Grapevine. You may also enjoy a round-trip journey from Grapevine to the Fort Worth Stockyards and back, which makes for a full day. Another option is a one-hour scenic trip across the Trinity River and back. Throughout the year, the GVVR offers special trips for Mother's Day, Father's Day, and many other occasions. Check out their website for full details.

705 S. Main St., Grapevine
817-410-3185
grapevinetexasusa.com/grapevine-vintage-railroad

SEE THE ONLY MICHELANGELO PAINTING
IN THE WESTERN HEMISPHERE AT THE KIMBELL ART MUSEUM

Fort Worth may be "where the West begins," but that doesn't stop it from having a sophisticated arts scene. Case in point: Fort Worth is home to the only Michelangelo painting in the Western Hemisphere. Michelangelo's *Torment of Saint Anthony* is filled with fascinating, yet creepy creatures and was created by Michelangelo Buonarroti around 1487 or 1488 when he was only twelve or thirteen years old. Although inspired by an engraving by Martin Schongauer, Michelangelo did more than just copy the other artist. He added interesting anatomical details, such as fish scales, to the flurry of demonic creatures seen pestering the saint. Michelangelo is known to have created only four paintings in his lifetime. *The Torment of Saint Anthony* is part of the Kimbell Art Museum's permanent collection, and viewing it is free to the public.

3333 Camp Bowie Blvd., Fort Worth
817-332-8451
kimbellart.org

BLAZE YOUR WAY
TO THE CHISHOLM TRAIL
OUTDOOR MUSEUM

The Chisholm Trail Outdoor Museum is a ten-acre park on the outskirts of Cleburne. In 1854, the town of Wardville stood here, creating an important stop for cattle drovers on their way to market. Nowadays, it's a great place to bring a packed lunch to enjoy at the covered picnic tables overlooking Lake Pat Cleburne. Afterward, you can explore several historic buildings on-site, including a log cabin courthouse, schoolhouse, jail, mercantile, herb gardens, teepees, and the Big Bear Native American Museum. A bright red stagecoach, which was used in two John Wayne movies, stands by the public restrooms. The museum hosts a variety of historic programs and hands-on workshops throughout the year. If you're lucky, the resident blacksmiths or other historic docents will be on-site when you visit.

101 Chisholm Trail, Cleburne
817-648-4633
jcchisholmtrail.com

GLIMPSE FORT WORTH'S ETERNAL LIGHT
AT THE STOCKYARDS MUSEUM

In 1970, the Guinness Book of World Records listed this Fort Worth light as the longest burning bulb in the world. Sadly, it was bumped to second place in 1973 by The Centennial Light, which burns in a Livermore, California, fire station, and boasts its own webcam. Even in second place, Fort Worth legendary light bulb is a marvel. Nicknamed the "Eternal Light," this historic light bulb has been burning since September 21, 1908. Now on view at the Fort Worth Stockyards Museum, where it is protected from the harsh Texas elements and kept on a protected electrical circuit, this little four-watt wonder just keeps on glowing.

131 E. Exchange Ave., Ste. 113, Fort Worth
817-625-5082
stockyardsmuseum.org

BE BLOWN AWAY
BY THE GONE WITH THE WIND REMEMBERED MUSEUM

After spending more than thirty years collecting memorabilia related to Margaret Mitchell's famous book and the movie it inspired, Vicky Rogers and her husband, Mike, created the Gone with the Wind Remembered Museum. Don't be fooled by the seemingly small size of the building. Once you step inside, you will be amazed by how much there is to see, including more than 650 dolls, original costumes, and an incredible array of foreign language versions of the book. Besides a Margaret Mitchell documentary, the movie *Gone with the Wind* plays on an endless loop in a little theater. Even if you don't consider yourself a *Gone with the Wind* fan, aka "Windie," you will be blown away by this well-organized and beautifully displayed private collection.

305 E. Second St., Cleburne
817-517-3897
gwtwremembered.com

STAND IN THE SHADE OF A HISTORIC BICENTENNIAL TREE
AT GREENWOOD MEMORIAL PARK

When Texas seceded from the Union during the Civil War, Charles Turner, a local farmer, merchant, and Texas Ranger, reluctantly went along with it, up to a point. Rather than exchange his entire fortune into Confederate notes, he buried $10,000 in gold beneath an old oak tree on his farm. After the Civil War, when Confederate notes were worthless, he dug up his buried treasure and then used it to help Fort Worth, a young city struggling to build its infrastructure and pay back Northern creditors. Mr. Turner is long gone, but that oak tree lives on. Besides having a role in the founding of Fort Worth, the Turner Oak is also a Bicentennial Tree, which means that it was alive when the United States Constitution was signed.

Greenwood Memorial Park
3100 White Settlement Rd., Fort Worth

SEE THE GUN THAT SHOT J.R.
AT SOUTHFORK RANCH

Southfork Ranch is a conference and event center with grounds that include a mansion made famous by the TV show *Dallas*. Fans of the series should be warned that only exterior shots of the Ewing family's ranch were shot here. Interiors were filmed in California. Even so, with longhorns and horses on the grounds, hardcore *Dallas* fans will enjoy the experience, which now includes sets and memorabilia from the 2012 TV series reboot. A guided tram tour shows you around the property. Afterward, you can tour a museum, which includes some props from the show, including the famous gun that shot J.R. Miss Ellie's Deli is the on-site eatery, and you can even buy designer Western duds and other souvenirs at the gift shops.

3700 Hogge Dr., Parker
972-442-7800
southforkranch.com

HIT THE ROAD
FOR THE DFW ELITE TOY MUSEUM

In the 1980s, businessman Ron Sturgeon began collecting antique toy cars. Eventually, his collection grew to such a point that he opened the DFW Elite Toy Museum to share it with others. While this unique museum is jam-packed with toys, the three thousand pieces currently on display represent only half of his collection. He keeps the other half at home! The exhibits feature model cars from all over the world, everything from scale models of historic street vehicles (Ford, Mercedes) to more exotic fare (Batmobile, Atom Jet Racer.) In addition to cars, you can find quirky items, such as old signs and salesman models. Not only is the DFW Elite Toy Museum free to the public, but it is also a dog-friendly space, which means the whole family is welcome, even Fido.

5940 Eden Dr., Fort Worth
817-834-3625
dfwelitetoymuseum.com

SHOPPING AND FASHION

CUSTOMIZE YOUR COWBOY STYLE
AT M.L. LEDDY'S

Traditional cowboy boots were designed for practical reasons. The heel is meant to grip stirrups, while the seventeen-inch height of the footwear protects the wearer's legs from all manner of wear and tear. These days, however, cowboy boots are more of a fashion statement for most of us, and while many stores throughout the DFW Metroplex carry cowboy boots, at M.L. Leddy's you can get a customized pair designed just to your liking and perfectly fitted to your body. Family owned and operated since it first opened in 1922, Leddy's is where the best-heeled cowboys and cowboy wannabes get their footwear. In addition to boots, Leddy's specializes in handmade saddles, belts, buckles, Western wear, and just about anything else you need to play cowboy.

2455 N. Main St., Fort Worth
817-624-3149
leddys.com

CRUISE THROUGH A THIRTY-MILE YARD SALE
DURING ANTIQUE ALLEY TEXAS

Each spring and fall, a cluster of north Texas towns unite to create a huge sale. Called Antique Alley Texas, this twice-yearly event stretches more than twenty-five miles and runs through the little towns of Cleburne and Sand Flat all the way to Maypearl and Grandview. Besides all sorts of antiques, artsy junk, and treasures, you will find food trucks offering everything from homemade ice create to slow-roasted BBQ. Antique Alley is a "rain or shine" event. The drive alone is worth the effort, since much of the journey takes you through tree-lined back roads and lush countryside. There's no telling what you will find along the way! Participating towns include Alvarado, Cleburne, Grandview, Maypearl, Keene, Sand Flat, Venus, and Waxahachie.

102 W. Main St. Grandview
940-867-6658
antiquealleytexas.com

LOOK FOR DECATUR GLASS
IN WISE COUNTY COURTHOUSE SQUARE

Decatur's Romanesque Revival–style courthouse was completed in 1896 and features pink granite with terra cotta accents. There is more to its design, however, than just good looks; the corner entrances keep air circulating and help cool the building. A variety of mom-and-pop shops surrounding the courthouse will keep you entertained for an afternoon. Keep an eye out for Decatur Glass in the antique stores. This handblown glass was produced in Decatur in the 1950s and 1960s at Tex Glass, Inc., a glass company started by husband and wife team, Bertha and Hermann Rosenzweig. Mr. Rosenzweig fled to the States after being persecuted by the Nazis. He eventually settled in Decatur and began producing a crinkle-style glassware. It's now a collectible unique to this region.

213 W. Main St., Decatur
940-704-7212
decaturtownsquare.com
decaturmainstreet.com

TIP: "EIGHTER FROM DECATUR"

If you gamble, you probably know the saying, "Eighter from Decatur, county seat of Wise." If you're not a gambler, you will definitely notice banners with "Eighter from Decatur" all over this little North Texas town.

In the late 1800s, a Decatur resident named Will Cooper fell in love with a gal named Ada. Every time he played craps, Mr. Cooper would chant, "Ada from Decatur, county seat of Wise." Before long, his catchy rhyme became popular and spread throughout the nation. Over time, "Ada" morphed into "Eighter," and in 1949, Decatur mayor Sly Hardwick added the phrase, "Eighter from Decatur" to the city's welcome signs, thereby securing its place in the local identity.

FIND A BARGAIN
AT FIRST MONDAY TRADE DAYS

Despite what the name implies, Weatherford's First Monday Trade Days is not held on the first Monday of the month. This flea market runs from 9:00 a.m. to 4:00 p.m. on the Friday, Saturday, and Sunday before the first Monday of each month. It's one of the oldest open-air markets in Texas and began in the mid-1800s when the Parker County Courthouse held legal trials at the start of each month. These proceedings attracted vendors, who would stand in the shade of the courthouse to sell their wares. This soon became a large open-air market, with ranchers, homesteaders, and other vendors buying, selling, and trading goods. The tradition continues into the new millennium, with a wide variety of goods, including livestock, antiques, farm-fresh produce, and even a gourmet food truck section.

317 Santa Fe Dr., Weatherford
817-598-4359
weatherfordparks.com/883/first-monday-trade-days

SHOP HUNGRY
AT THE DALLAS FARMERS MARKET

Make sure you've got walking shoes on because in true Texas form the Dallas Farmers Market is big. Shop early for the best selection, and shop late for the best deals. For locally grown produce, look for the yellow "certified local" sign. Most vendors take cash only, so don't bring big bills. The indoor section of the Dallas Farmers Market is a good place to grab a bite to eat and cool off since it's air-conditioned. This is also where you find a variety of specialty food vendors: hormone-free meats, organic tea and coffee, smoked sausage, Texas olive oil, and much, much, more. Check out the official website for a list of what is currently in season, or simply head on down to see what's fresh today.

920 S. Harwood St., Dallas
469-607-5899
dallasfarmersmarket.org

SEE WHY MCKINNEY
IS UNIQUE BY NATURE

McKinney is a booming bedroom community that combines urban convenience with small-town charm and regularly makes its way onto lists of the best places to live in the DFW Metroplex. A Neoclassical Revival limestone courthouse (which now houses the McKinney Performing Arts Center) sits at the heart of the historic town square, where it's surrounded by antique stores, boutiques, restaurants, and other shops. After you've perused the square, drop by the Landon Winery or commune with nature at the 289-acre Heard Natural Science Museum. Remember to keep an eye on the McKinney website to plan ahead for the April Arts in Bloom, the McKinney Oktoberfest, and other special events throughout the year.

McKinney Performing Arts Center
111 N. Tennessee St., McKinney
972-547-2650
mckinneytexas.org

Heard Natural Science Museum
1 Nature Pl., McKinney
972-562-5566
heardmuseum.org

Landon Winery
101 N. Kentucky St., McKinney
972-542-3030
landonwinery.com

FIND A PAGE-TURNER
AT HALF PRICE BOOKS' FLAGSHIP STORE

From its humble beginnings as a used bookstore in an old laundromat, Half Price Books (HPB) has expanded to more than 120 stores, making it the largest family-owned bookstore in the USA. As they put it, "We buy and sell everything ever printed or recorded (except yesterday's newspaper)."

In addition to selling books, HPB is committed to promoting literacy and participates in the Million Book Project, which donates books to qualifying nonprofits and schools. The flagship store in Dallas, where it all began in 1972, spans fifty-five thousand square feet and remains an excellent place to buy used books, movies, music (vinyl and CD), and more. You can even grab an espresso or lunch at the in-store Black Forest Café.

5803 E. Northwest Hwy., Dallas
214-379-8000
hpb.com

SEEK OUT UNIQUE DEALS
AT TRADERS VILLAGE

Of all the weekend flea markets in the DFW area, Traders Village is the biggest. Every Saturday and Sunday in Grand Prairie this eclectic open-air flea market offers clothing, furniture, jewelry, knickknacks, fruits and veg, home decor, electronics, purses, toys, tires, wheels, boots, and more for sale. You can find some unique treasures here, and many vendors will haggle over the price. In addition to all the items for sale, Traders Village hosts a variety of festivals throughout the year, including Native American powwows, auto shows, Cajun fests, Comicons, Cinco de Mayo Celebrations, and more. If you're with the children, drop by the carnival rides. While admission is free, parking is $4 per car. The lot is huge, too, so remember where you parked!

2602 Mayfield Rd., Grand Prairie
972-647-2331
tradersvillage.com

START YOUR EXPLORATION OF PETRIFIED CITY
AT SOMERVELL COURTHOUSE SQUARE

In its heyday, the town of Glen Rose was nicknamed "Petrified City" due to the abundance of buildings here with petrified wood exteriors. Roughly forty of these eye-catching structures remain, considerably more than any other Texas town. The Somerville Courthouse is a stately limestone building in the heart of town. A small park in front of the courthouse features a gazebo and star-shaped water fountain, both of which are constructed from local petrified wood, crystals, and fossilized dinosaur footprints. A variety of restaurants, antique shops, and boutiques line the square, which makes a fun stop after visiting local sights, such as Fossil Rim Park and Dinosaur Valley State Park. While you're there, drop by the StorieBook Café. This charming bookstore/café is a short walk from the town square.

Somervell Courthouse Square
101 NE Barnard St., Glen Rose
254-897-3081
glenrosetexas.net/219/historic-courthouse-square

StorieBook Café
502 SW Barnard St., Glen Rose
254-897-2665

FLIP YOUR LID
FOR PETERS BROTHERS HATS

Greek immigrants Jim and Tom Peters opened this iconic hat store in 1911, and it's still proudly family-owned to this day. After studying the art of haberdashery with none other than Jim Stetson, the brothers began producing their own line of hats, including the iconic "Shady Oaks" style, which has been given to prestigious guests of Fort Worth, including John F. Kennedy on his fateful visit in 1963. During World War II and through the Korean War, the brothers even made hats for the US military. Peters Brothers Hats offers custom-made hats, along with a wide variety of fedoras, Western hats, and more. They also repair damaged hats, so if you inherited a dinged up derby from your grandpa, you can have it restored here.

909 Houston St., Fort Worth
817-335-1715
pbhats.com

FIND HIDDEN TREASURES
AT MONTGOMERY ANTIQUE STORE & TEAROOM

This Texas-sized antique mall features booths from more than two hundred different dealers. Keep your cell phone ringer on because it's easy to lose friends and family in the labyrinthine rows of antiques. Most pieces for sale are mid-century or older, but this is interspersed with a few modern craft items, such as handmade soaps, clothing created from repurposed fabric, steampunk lamps, quilts, and crocheted items. When it's too hot to stretch your legs outside, you can log a few steps at the Montgomery Antique Store in air-conditioned comfort and perhaps find the perfect treasure to take home along the way. In the middle of this maze, you will find a quaintly decorated tearoom offering sandwiches, quiche, scones, and refreshing mango iced tea.

2601 Montgomery St., Fort Worth
817-735-9685
montgomerystreetantiques.com

WANDER THROUGH COLORFUL STALLS
AT HENDERSON STREET BAZAAR

This lively Hispanic flea market is especially colorful on Sunday afternoons when the after-church crowd comes here for a family stroll. Covered stalls offer much-needed shade in the summer months, and as you wander the crowded booths, you'll hear music wafting through the grounds, everything from rowdy pop hits and Latino ballads to live accordion music played by strolling musicians. Items for sale run the gamut from fresh produce, candy, housewares, clothing, cowboy boots, furniture, and Western wear to car supplies, plants, gardening supplies, shoes, toiletries, school supplies, Mexican Coca-Cola, and more. There's a food court near the center offering treats such as quesadillas, tacos, elotes, snow cones, nachos, and other fast-food items. Many vendors will barter, and if you speak Spanish, it's a plus.

1000 N. Henderson St., Fort Worth
817-877-3021

SHOP LOCAL
AT HISTORIC GRANBURY SQUARE

Granbury is a small but lively town that hosts one festival after another throughout the year, including a kite festival, a Texas Independence Day Celebration, a Wine Walk, a Warriors for Christ biker rally, a literary festival, the Langdon Review Weekend, and the Granbury Paranormal Expo, among many others. Most of these events center around Granbury's native limestone courthouse, which is a fine example of French Empire–style architecture and dates to 1891. The town is worth a visit even during non-festival days, since the courthouse is ringed with an array of boutiques, restaurants, wine bars, art galleries, and cafés. During festivals, the town square turns into an outdoor fair, with bandstands and booths selling art, crafts, and food.

100 E. Pearl St., Granbury
682-936-4550
granburysquare.com

POP IN FOR POPOVERS
AT THE NIEMAN MARCUS
FLAGSHIP STORE

Nieman Marcus was founded in 1907, and its flagship store in Dallas is the last of the city's original department stores. Neiman Marcus made a name for itself selling high-end luxury goods, designer clothing brands, expensive jewelry, and other upscale offerings. Unlike other Neiman Marcus stores in the area, this one includes a bridal shop. The company briefly considered relocating to a shopping mall during the 1980s but decided to remain in this historic locale. Lunching on the sixth floor restaurant, the Zodiac, is a special experience, with linen table cloths, a quiet dining room, and old-school elegance. Diners are treated to a dainty cheese biscuit and broth as well as complimentary popovers with strawberry butter before the meal.

1618 Main St., Dallas 75201
214-573-5800
neimanmarcus.com/stores/dallas/tx/dallas%20-%20downtown

GO ANTIQUING
AT THE WAXAHACHIE HISTORIC COURTHOUSE SQUARE

Although the Texas State Legislature deemed Waxahachie the Crape Myrtle Capital of Texas, this quaint town is also known as the Movie Capital of Texas (with more than thirty filmed here) and the Gingerbread City (due to its abundance of ornately decorated Victorian homes). Waxahachie hosts festivals throughout the year, including the Scarborough Renaissance Festival in May, the Gingerbread Trail in June, the Crape Myrtle Festival in July, and a World War II Reenactment for Veterans Day in November, among others. You'll find the Ellis County Courthouse in the heart of Waxahachie's historic downtown. This Romanesque Revival beauty stands nine stories high and includes both gray and pink granite as well as red sandstone. This shopping area includes antique stores, specialty shops, gift stores, and restaurants, and is close to the local farmers market.

Waxahachie Historic Courthouse Square
101 W. Main St., Waxahachie
waxahachiecvb.com

Waxahachie Downtown Farmers Market
410 S. Rogers St., Waxahachie ·
469-309-4111
waxahachiecvb.com/business/waxahachie-downtown-farmers-market

TIP

In the 1980s, Hollywood discovered Waxahachie and used its historic buildings as the backdrop for several movies, including three Academy Award winners, *Tender Mercies* (starring Robert Duvall), *The Trip to Bountiful* (starring Geraldine Page), and *Places in the Heart* (starring Sally Field, John Malkovich, and Danny Glover). In addition, several episodes of the TV show *Walker, Texas Ranger* (starring Chuck Norris) were filmed in Waxahachie.

PLACE YOUR BID
AT THE TEXAS STAR AUCTIONS

For a truly unique shopping experience, head to Texas Star Auctions in Haltom City. This family-owned-and-operated business conducts sales events with professional auctioneers throughout the year. Although wholesalers often fill the seats, these auctions are open to the public, which means anyone can come and find a deal. Items run the gamut from estate sale antiques and mid-century collectibles to truly one-of-a-kind items. You can even place your own objects for sale through them by consignment. While you also have the option to place absentee bids or make purchases while watching the online simulcast, you really need to see Texas Star Auctions in person at least once. Even if you don't buy anything, it's worth it to marvel at these fast-talking auctioneers.

2301 Solona St., Haltom City
817-744-7772
texasstarauctions.com

FIND FRESH AND EXOTIC INGREDIENTS
AT NGUYEN LOI ORIENTAL SUPERMARKET

Nguyen Loi Oriental Supermarket in Haltom City offers a wide array of specialty ingredients for Asian cuisine as well as great deals on coconut milk, tea, rice, ramen, coffee, and fresh produce. Some folks may be surprised by the seafood section, which includes a large tank full of live blue crabs, lobsters, catfish, and other sea creatures, depending on the season. In addition to chicken eggs, the dairy section offers duck and quail eggs. If you are not familiar with Asian cooking, you will find lots of unusual items and new things to try, such as chicken feet, lychee nuts, and roast duck. With ample parking out front and several Asian restaurants within walking distance, why not grab lunch nearby before you go in and shop?

5302 E. Belknap St., Ste. C, Haltom City
817-831-4778

WINDOW-SHOP 'TIL YOU DROP
AT THE DALLAS MARKET CENTER

Simply put, the Dallas Market Center is huge. We're talking five million square feet! Everything from shoes, flowers, home decor, and apparel to bridal wear, housewares, and more is spread across four separate buildings: the World Trade Center, the Plaza, the Trade Mart, and the Market Hall. Altogether, roughly twenty-three hundred showrooms highlighting goods from all over the world are showcased throughout the Dallas Market Center compound. Although this massive marketplace caters to wholesale buyers rather than casual retail shoppers, the Dallas Market Center hosts several events that are open to the public throughout the year, including a bridal fair, pet expo, dog show, guitar fest, boat show, used book sales, and more.

2100 N. Stemmons Freeway, Dallas
214-655-6100
dallasmarketcenter.com/public

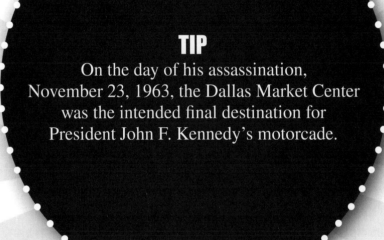

TIP
On the day of his assassination,
November 23, 1963, the Dallas Market Center
was the intended final destination for
President John F. Kennedy's motorcade.

SHOP, STROLL, AND EAT
YOUR WAY AROUND
DENTON'S COURTHOUSE-ON-THE-SQUARE

Built in 1896 using native Texas limestone, Denton's Courthouse-on-the-Square is a gorgeous Romanesque Revival–style building that's listed on the National Register of Historic Places. Although the courthouse houses several county offices, it also has a free museum dedicated to local history that is worth a visit. This grand structure is surrounded by locally owned eateries, shops, and cafés, some of which have been in business since the 1940s. The square is the focal point for festivities throughout the year and is especially pretty during the annual Denton Holiday Lighting Festival in the fall, when all the trees and buildings are draped in white lights. In May and June, musicians perform live music in a series of concerts on the courthouse lawn.

110 W. Hickory St., Denton
940-349-2850
dentoncounty.com/Departments/History-and-Culture/Office-of-History-and-Culture/VISIT.aspx

FIND A LITTLE OF EVERYTHING
AT BEN FRANKLIN APOTHECARY

Since 1964 Ben Franklin Apothecary has been a family-owned general store and independent pharmacy. More than fifty years later, this Duncanville variety store continues to thrive. In addition to the general store and gift shop, Ben Franklin Apothecary includes an old-fashioned deli and soda fountain. The pharmacy section includes a wide selection of items for diabetics, and they carry a lot of specialty medical supplies. The venue also includes a quilting and sewing section, where you can find a big selection of fabric and notions as well as sewing and quilting classes. Between enjoying lunch in the '50s style diner and perusing the wares, you can easily spend an entire afternoon here.

302 N. Main St., Duncanville
972-298-1147
benfranklinrx.com

SUGGESTED
ITINERARIES

ANTIQUES & FLEA MARKETS

DATE NIGHT

FESTIVALS GALORE

FREE FAMILY FUN

ONLY IN TEXAS

GREAT OUTDOORS

HISTORIC TOWN SQUARES

RAINY DAY FUN

ACTIVITIES
BY SEASON

SPRING

Cruise through a Thirty-Mile Yard Sale During Antique Alley Texas, 103

Explore Deep Ellum for Eclectic and Artsy Big D Fun, 41

Take Time to Smell the Flowers on the Ennis Bluebonnet Trails, 62

Swing into the Spring at the Annual Jazz Age Sunday Social, 47

Czech Out the National Polka Festival in Ennis, 40

Party Like It's 1533 at Scarborough Renaissance Festival, 29

Admire the Craftsmanship at Wood, Waves, and Wheels, 61

SUMMER

Have a Bang-Up Time at Addison Kaboom Town!, 34

Delight in Old-Fashioned Swimming Hole at Burger's Lake, 58

Marvel at Rodeo Riding and Roping Skills in Fort Worth and Mesquite, 63

Feast at a Table Set for 300 at Plano's Night Out On 15th Street, 6

FALL

WINTER

INDEX

• •

• •

• •